Full STEAM Ahead!
Arts in Action

# How Do Artists Tell Stories?

## Robin Johnson

CRABTREE
PUBLISHING COMPANY
WWW.CRABTREEBOOKS.COM

## Title-Specific Learning Objectives:

Readers will:

- Identify and understand how the author supports ideas with reasons.
- Explain that artists tell stories in their art, and that the stories can make people feel different ways.
- Describe some of the ways artists tell stories, such as using color, symbols, or sound.

| High-frequency words (grade one)<br>and, can, has, is, make, play, tell, they, to | Academic vocabulary<br>characters, plot, quilt, setting, statue, symbol |
|---|---|

## Before, During, and After Reading Prompts:

### Activate Prior Knowledge and Make Predictions:
Have children read the title and look at the cover images. Ask:

- What do you think the book will be about?
- What do you know about stories?
- Why do people tell stories?
- What is the last story you read?

### During Reading:
After reading page 8, have children focus on the painting there. Ask them:

- What story is the picture telling us?

- Who are the characters? What is the setting? (Encourage children to refer to the caption when answering these questions.)
- What could the story be about? (Encourage children to make text-to-self connections.)

### After Reading:
Show children pictures of symbols and share what they think they mean. Use the symbols to represent the plot of a familiar story.

Play snippets of music for children. Have them act out the feeling or story that the music is telling.

**Author:** Robin Johnson

**Series Development:** Reagan Miller

**Editor:** Janine Deschenes

**Proofreader:** Melissa Boyce

**STEAM Notes for Educators:** Reagan Miller and Janine Deschenes

**Guided Reading Leveling:** Publishing Solutions Group

**Cover, Interior Design, and Prepress:** Samara Parent

**Photo research:** Robin Johnson and Samara Parent

**Production coordinator:** Katherine Berti

**Photographs:**
iStock: catnap72: p. 13 (top)
Shutterstock: Pavel L Photo and Video: front cover; 501room: title page; Anton_Ivanov: p. 5 (top); Alain Lauga: p. 10; Solodov Aleksei: p. 12; lazyllama: p. 15; Igor Bulgarin: p. 16; Kamira: p. 19 (top); tarczas: p. 21
All other photographs by Shutterstock

### Library and Archives Canada Cataloguing in Publication

Johnson, Robin (Robin R.) author
    How do artists tell stories? / Robin Johnson.

(Full STEAM ahead!)
Includes index.
Issued in print and electronic formats.
ISBN 978-0-7787-6211-9 (hardcover).--
ISBN 978-0-7787-6270-6 (softcover).--ISBN 978-1-4271-2267-4 (HTML)

        1. Emotions in art--Juvenile literature. 2. Emotions in music--Juvenile literature. 3. Emotions in dance--Juvenile literature.
4. Storytelling in art--Juvenile literature. 5. Storytelling--Juvenile literature. I. Title.

NX650 E46 J64 2019          j700'.4353          C2018-906201-0
                                                C2018-906202-9

### Library of Congress Cataloging-in-Publication Data

Names: Johnson, Robin (Robin R.), author.
Title: How do artists tell stories? / Robin Johnson.
Description: New York : Crabtree Publishing Company, 2019. | Series: Full STEAM ahead! | Includes index.
Identifiers: LCCN 2018056601 (print) | LCCN 2018057240 (ebook) | ISBN 9781427122674 (Electronic) | ISBN 9780778762119 (hardcover : alk. paper) | ISBN 9780778762706 (pbk. : alk. paper)
Subjects: LCSH: Arts--Psychology--Juvenile literature.
Classification: LCC NX165 (ebook) | LCC NX165 .J64 2019 (print) | DDC 700.1/9--dc23
LC record available at https://lccn.loc.gov/2018056601

Printed in the U.S.A./042019/CG20190215

# Table of Contents

## Crabtree Publishing Company

www.crabtreebooks.com .......................... 1-800-387-7650

**Published in Canada**
**Crabtree Publishing**
616 Welland Ave.
St. Catharines, Ontario
L2M 5V6

**Published in the United States**
**Crabtree Publishing**
PMB 59051
350 Fifth Avenue, 59th Floor
New York, New York 10118

**Published in the United Kingdom**
**Crabtree Publishing**
Maritime House
Basin Road North, Hove
BN41 1WR

**Published in Australia**
**Crabtree Publishing**
Unit 3 – 5 Currumbin Court
Capalaba
QLD 4157

# What is an Artist?

An artist is a person who makes art. Artists make pictures. They make pots and **statues**. They also dance, sing, act, and make music.

This artist is making a pot. She shapes it with her hands.

Museums are places
people visit to see art.

These artists are dancing
and playing music.

# What are Stories?

Stories tell us about people and places. We read stories in books. We watch them in movies. We hear them from others.

A story has characters. They can be people and animals. A story has a setting. A setting is the place and time of the story.

A story has a plot. A plot is the events that make up the story. The plot of this story tells about a dog who saves his friends.

# Artists Tell Stories

Artists tell stories in the art they make. Art can have characters, settings, and plots.

This painting tells a story about children and a dog playing in the snow. The setting is a backyard in winter.

This artist writes a song on her **computer**. The song tells a story about spring.

# Many Stories

Artists tell many kinds of stories.
Some stories are happy. Others are sad.
Artists show feelings in different ways.

This artist acts in a **play**. She cries to show that her character is sad.

Some artists take photos with tools called **cameras**. This artist takes a photo of his dog playing. The photo tells a happy story.

# Symbols Tell Stories

Artists can use symbols to tell stories. Symbols are pictures that have different meanings. A heart is a symbol that means love.

This statue shows a girl holding a dove. A dove is a symbol that means peace.

Some artists make **quilts**. Many quilts have symbols. This quilt shows a house. A house is a symbol that means family.

This painting shows a lion. A lion is a symbol that means strength.

# Pictures Tell Stories

Artists tell stories in the pictures they make. They use colors to show different feelings. Bright colors can show happy or excited feelings. Dark colors can show sad feelings.

This drawing shows a girl standing alone.
The artist used dark colors to show that she feels sad.

This painting shows people at a party. The artist used bright colors to show that they feel happy.

# Actors Tell Stories

Some artists tell stories by acting like characters. They are actors. They use words and actions to tell stories. They use their faces to show how the characters feel.

costumes

rock

trees

These actors use **costumes** to look like different characters. A rock and trees show the setting of the story.

Actors called **mimes** do not use words. They tell stories with their actions. They use their faces to show how their characters feel.

# Music Tells Stories

Some artists make music. They sing songs. They make sounds with **instruments**. They tell stories with their music.

This artist sings a song. The words in the song tell a story.

trumpet

Artists make loud and soft sounds to show different feelings. Trumpets make loud sounds. They can show excited feelings.

Artists change the speed of their music to tell different stories. Slow music might tell a sad story. Fast music might tell a happy story.

# Dancers Tell Stories

Dancers tell stories by moving their bodies. They move to the sound of music. The ways that they move show how they are feeling.

These dancers jump up and down. They move to fast music. They tell a happy story.

These artists dance together. They move to slow music. They tell a story about two people who love each other.

# Words to Know

**cameras** [KAM-er-*uh*s] noun  A tool that takes pictures or videos

**computer** [k*uh*m-PYOO-ter] noun  An electronic device that does a job

**costumes** [KOS-tooms] noun  Things people wear to look like different characters

**instruments** [IN-str*uh*-m*uh*nts] noun  Tools that make musical sounds

**mimes** [mahyms] noun  Actors who do not use words

**play** [pley] noun  A show that people watch

**quilts** [kwilts] noun  Blankets made up of patches

**statues** [STACH-oos] noun  A type of 3-D art made of materials in different shapes

A noun is a person, place, or thing.
A verb is an action word that tells you what someone or something does.
An adjective is a word that tells you what something is like.

# Index

## About the Author

Robin Johnson is a freelance author and editor who has written more than 80 children's books. When she isn't working, Robin builds castles in the sky with her engineer husband and their two best creations—sons Jeremy and Drew.

To explore and learn more, enter the code at the Crabtree Plus website below.

www.crabtreeplus.com/fullsteamahead

Your code is:
fsa20

23

# STEAM Notes for Educators

Full STEAM Ahead is a literacy series that helps readers build vocabulary, fluency, and comprehension while learning about big ideas in STEAM subjects. *How Do Artists Tell Stories* helps readers learn how an author supports ideas with reasons, connecting claims in the text with images of art. The STEAM activity below helps readers extend the ideas in the book to build their skills in visual and language arts.

## Telling My Story

Children will be able to:
- Understand and identify how art tells a story.
- Create a coat of arms that tells their story.
- Explain how their art tells a story about themselves.

### Materials
- My Coat of Arms Worksheet
- My Coat of Arms Completed Example
- Drawing and coloring materials

### Guiding Prompts
After reading *How do Artists Tell Stories*, ask:
- What are the parts of a story?
- How can art tell a story? What elements of art help tell stories? (Color, symbols, etc.)

### Activity Prompts
Review pages 12 to 15 with children. Ask them:
- Can you think of a symbol that tells a story?
- What do artists use to tell stories in pictures?

Explain to children that they will create art that tells a story about who they are!
- Show children My Coat of Arms Completed Example to spark interest.

Explain to children that a coat of arms is a design that uses pictures and symbols to give information about a family.

Hand children My Coat of Arms Worksheet and Completed Example. Have them follow the instructions to draw and color symbols and pictures that tell a story about themselves.

Have children answer the question at the bottom of the worksheet. The question asks them to explain how their art tells a story about themselves.

Invite children to present their coat of arms. Then, display them on a classroom wall.

### Extensions
- Have children tell a story about their first day of school using one other type of art, such as music, acting, miming, sculpture, etc.

To view and download the worksheets, visit **www.crabtreebooks.com/resources/printables** or **www.crabtreeplus.com/fullsteamahead** and enter the code **fsa20**.